CODE BREAKER

Use the codes below to help answer the code breaker questions within the workbook

A	J	S			
B	K	T			
C	L	U			
D	M 	V			
E	N	W			
F	O	X			
G	P	Y			
H	Q	Z			
I	R				

CONTENTS

Juz 1 | **Allah & the angels** 06

Juz 2 | **Talut & his people** 10

Juz 3 | **Ibrahim & the King** 14

Juz 4 | **Story of Abu Bakr** 18

Juz 5 | **The people of the Saturday** 22

Juz 6 | **The sons of Adam** 26

Juz 7 | **Allah & Eesa** 30

Juz 8 | **The people of Jannah & Jahanum** 34

Juz 9 | **Musa & the magicians** 38

Juz 10 | **Story of Ka'b ibn Malik** 42

Juz 11 | **Musa & Firawn** 46

Juz 12 | **Nuh & his sons** 50

Juz 13 | **Ya'qub & his sons** 54

Juz 14 | **Ibrahim & the angels** 58

Juz 15 | **Musa & Khidr** 62

Juz 16 | **Allah & Musa** 66

Juz 17 | **Ibrahim & the idols** 70

Juz 18 | **Allah & the Quran** 74

Juz 19 | **Sulaiman and the hud hud** 78

Juz 20 | **Musa's mother** 82

Juz 21 | **Luqman & his son** 86

Juz 22 | **The 3 Messengers** 90

Juz 23 | **Ibrahim & Ismail** 94

Juz 24 | **The believer from Firawn's family** 98

Juz 25 | **Muhammad ﷺ & the Quraysh** 102

Juz 26 | **Hud** 106

Juz 27 | **The hypocrites** 110

Juz 28 | **Muhammad ﷺ & the hypocrites** 114

Juz 29 | **Nuh & his people** 118

Juz 30 | **The first revelation** 122

Reward Chart

Dearest viewers, welcome to your new workbook!

There are 30 worksheets you need to complete, you can find the answers for each worksheet based on every episode of The Azharis. Every worksheet will help you learn a new story from each Juz of the Quran.

Once you have completed the worksheet find the correct sticker on the sticker page (found at the end of the workbook) and stick it in the matching circle, or you can colour it in.

Episode 01 Episode 02 Episode 03 Episode 04 Episode 05
Juz 1   Juz 2   Juz 3   Juz 4   Juz 5

Episode 06 Episode 07 Episode 08 Episode 09 Episode 10
Juz 6   Juz 7   Juz 8   Juz 9   Juz 10

Episode 11   Episode 12   Episode 13   Episode 14   Episode 15
Juz 11   Juz 12   Juz 13   Juz 14   Juz 15

Don't forget!
On completion of episodes **10**, **20** and **30** you are able to download your achievement certificates from
www.theazharis.com

Episode 16
Juz 16

Episode 17
Juz 17

Episode 18
Juz 18

Episode 19
Juz 19

Episode 20
Juz 20

Episode 21
Juz 21

Episode 22
Juz 22

Episode 23
Juz 23

Episode 24
Juz 24

Episode 25
Juz 25

Episode 26
Juz 26

Episode 27
Juz 27

Episode 28
Juz 28

Episode 29
Juz 29

Episode 30
Juz 30

The Azharis | Juz by Juz Stories 05

JUZ 1
Allah & the angels

1. What did Allah create Prophet Adam from?

Circle the correct answer

Earth

Fire

2. What was the first thing that Prophet Adam did?

Join the dots

SNEEZED

3. What should we say when we sneeze?

Break the code | Refer to the code breaker sheet at the end of the workbook

___ ___ ___ ___ ___ ___ ___ ___ ___ ___ ___ ___

4. What happens when we shake hands?

Write the answer and colour in

_____

_____

_____

_____

5. Whose bright face did Prophet Adam see?

Colour in

6. How many years did Prophet Dawud live for?

Circle the correct answer

360 years   60 years   100 years   150 years   40 years   230 years

JUZ 1

7. What did Prophet Adam forget?

Write the answer

_____

_____

_____

COMPETITION TIME!

Watch the Juz 1 episode for the questions

Circle the correct answer

Each correct answer is worth 2 points, leaving you with a total score out of 6

Lets see if you can beat The Azharis!

Question	Answer		Score
	(Circle the correct answer)		
1	Ramadan	Sha'ban	
2	10	30	
3	Surah Al Fatiha	Surah Al Alaq	
Total Score			/6

JUZ 1

THE AZHARI PAD

Watch the Juz 1 episode for the questions

1

2

Draw: 1. When we greet each other what should we shake? 2. A picture of your heart.

The Azharis | Juz by Juz Stories 09

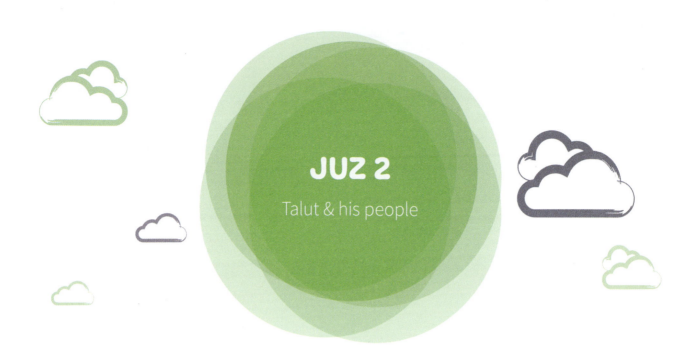

JUZ 2
Talut & his people

1. If you really want something, what should you do?

Unscramble the words below

KAME UDA

2. The people of Talut didn't like him because he was…

Fill in the gap

3. Does having money automatically mean you are a good person?

Find your way to the correct answer

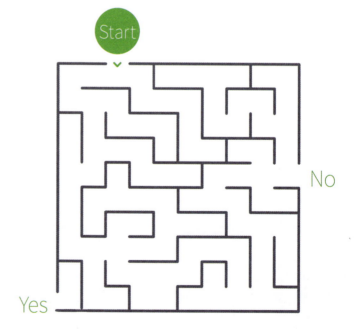

4. What happened to the box when put under the statues in the morning?

Write the answer and colour in

_____

_____

_____

_____

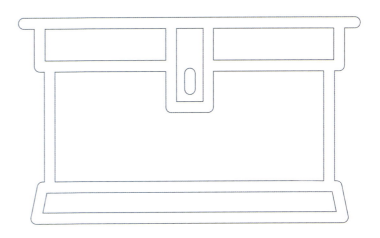

5. Around how many people were left in the army?

Circle the correct answer

400 People

220 People

310 People

150 People

30 People

230 People

JUZ 2

6. Who was the young boy in the story?

Join the dots

DAWUD

_____

COMPETITION TIME!

Watch the Juz 2 episode for the questions

Circle the correct answer

Each correct answer is worth 2 points, leaving you with a total score out of 6

Lets see if you can beat The Azharis!

Question	Answer (Circle the correct answer)		Score
1	Muhammad ﷺ	Musa	
2	Surah Al Fatiha	Surah Al Iklhas	
3	Surah Al Mulk	Surah Al Kahf	
	Total Score		/6

JUZ 2

THE AZHARI PAD

Watch the Juz 2 episode for the questions

Draw: 1. If you had lots of money, what would you buy? **2.** The part that wasn't covered.

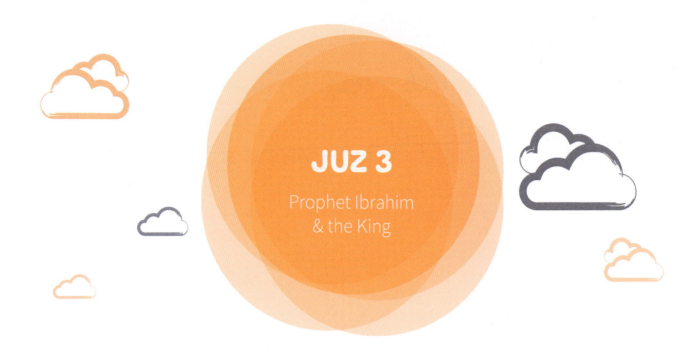

JUZ 3
Prophet Ibrahim & the King

1. Write something that only Allah can do.

Write the answer

_____

_____

_____

2. The thing Prophet Ibrahim said that the King could not move was the _____.

Fill in the gap and colour in

3. Is it good to argue?

Colour in the correct answer

4. What animal did he have?

Complete the dot to dot and write the answer

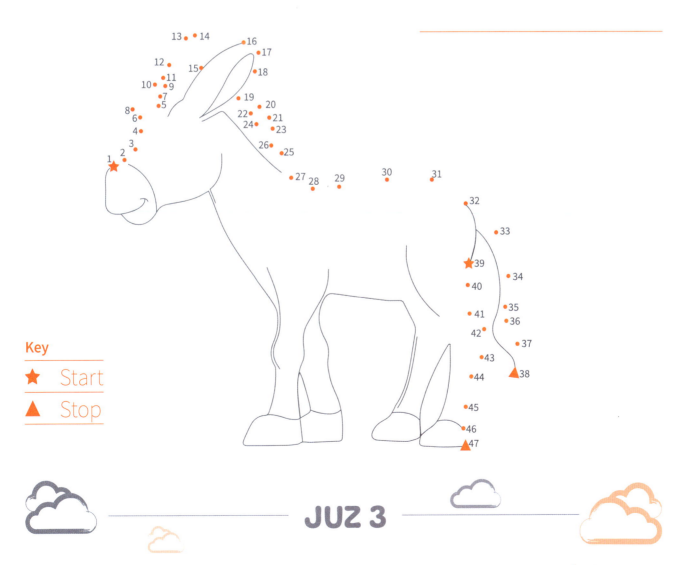

Key
★ Start
▲ Stop

JUZ 3

5. How many years was Uzayr asleep for?

Circle the correct answer

10 years   20 years   100 years   220 years   300 years   150 years

COMPETITION TIME!

Watch the Juz 3 episode for the questions

Circle the correct answer

Each correct answer is worth 2 points, leaving you with a total score out of 6

Lets see if you can beat The Azharis!

Question	Answer (Circle the correct answer)		Score
1	Muhammad ﷺ	Adam	
2	Surah Al Fatiha	Surah An Nas	
3	4	2	
Total Score			/6

JUZ 3

THE AZHARI PAD

Watch the Juz 3 episode for the questions

Draw: 1. What do kings wear on their heads? 2. What food do you think he had?

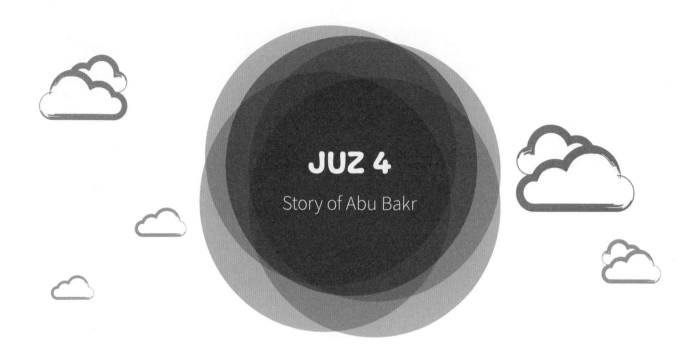

JUZ 4
Story of Abu Bakr

1. How many gates are there to Jannah?

Write the answer

_____

2. Who did the Prophet ﷺ say he hoped would be called from all the gates?

Join the dots

ABU BAKR

3. Who competed with Abu Bakr?

Break the code | Refer to the code breaker sheet at the end of the workbook

____ ____ ____ ____

4. What happened with the Prophet ﷺ when he went into the cave?

Write the answer

_____

_____

_____

Wordsearch

Tick off the words as you find them

- ○ MECCA
- ○ UMAR
- ○ CAVE
- ○ QURAN

E	C	M	C	T	Q
F	A	A	R	D	U
U	V	S	V	E	R
M	E	C	C	A	A
A	R	S	M	L	N
R	C	Q	Q	P	Z

JUZ 4

5. On what day did the Prophet ﷺ die?

Colour in

MONDAY

COMPETITION TIME!

Watch the Juz 4 episode for the questions

Circle the correct answer

Each correct answer is worth 2 points, leaving you with a total score out of 6

Lets see if you can beat The Azharis!

Question	Answer (Circle the correct answer)		Score
1	40	63	
2	Mecca	Medinah	
3	Hira	Thawr	
Total Score			/6

JUZ 4

The Azharis | Juz by Juz Stories 20

THE AZHARI PAD

Watch the Juz 4 episode for the questions

1

2

Draw: 1. An example of doing something to help someone. **2.** Something in Mecca.

JUZ 5
The people of the Saturday

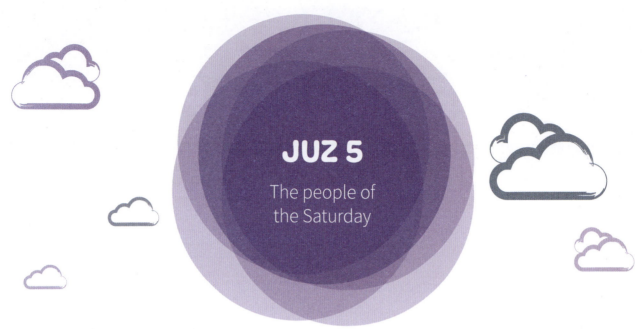

1. What was their test?

Write the answer

_____
_____

2. _____ taught the fish which day it was.

Fill in the gap and colour in

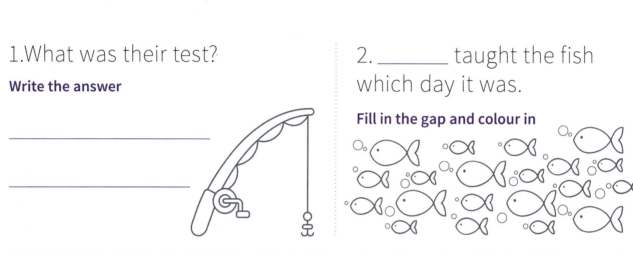

3. Which day of the week is Jummah?

Circle the correct answer

Friday   Saturday

4. What did the tree do when the Prophet ﷺ left it?

Write the answer

_____
_____

5. Is it good to help others?

Find your way to the correct answer

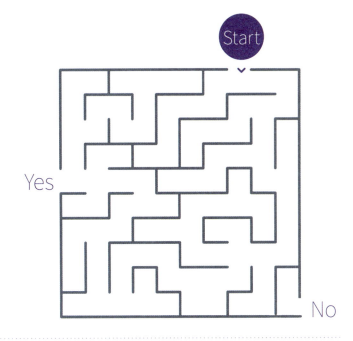

6. Draw an example of how you can help someone.

Draw

7. Were the group that didn't do anything and kept quiet saved?

Colour in the correct answer

YES | NO

COMPETITION TIME!

Watch the Juz 5 episode for the questions

Circle the correct answer

Each correct answer is worth 2 points, leaving you with a total score out of 6

Lets see if you can beat The Azharis!

Question	Answer		Score
	(Circle the correct answer)		
1	Surah Al Fatiha	Ayatul Kursi	
2	Surah Al Ikhlas	Surah Al Kawthar	
3	Surah Al Baqarah	Surah Al Imran	
Total Score			/6

JUZ 5

THE AZHARI PAD

Watch the Juz 5 episode for the question

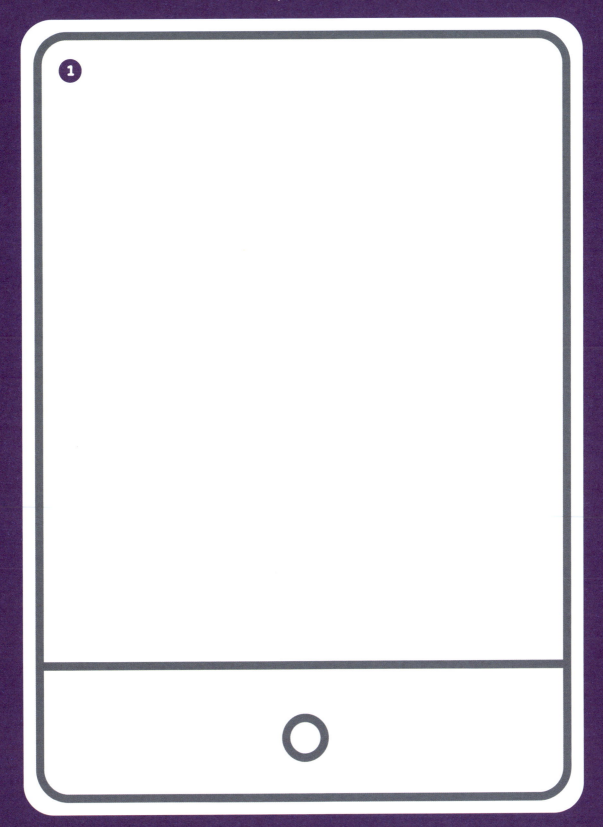

Draw: 1. What do you need to use to catch fish?

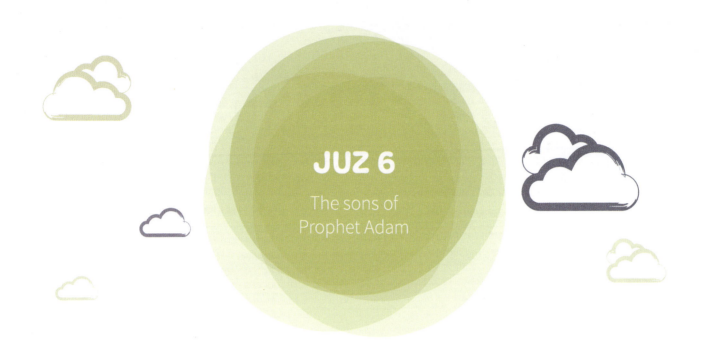

JUZ 6
The sons of Prophet Adam

1. Which is not the name of one of Prophet Adam's sons?
Circle the correct answer

Habil Qabil Sabil

2. What was the sign that the sacrifice was not accepted?
Write the answer and colour in

_____

_____

_____

3. If we get angry what should we say?
Colour in

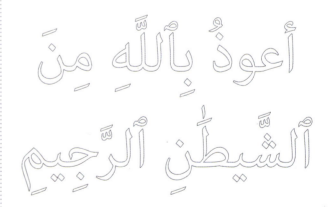

Audhubillahi min ashaytan ar-rajeem (Bukhari)

4. Ihsan is doing things to the _____ of your _____ .

Fill in the gaps and colour in

5. What does it mean to be jealous?

Write the answer

_____
_____
_____

6. Which animal did Allah send as a sign?

Complete the dot to dot and write the answer

Key
★ Start
▲ Stop

JUZ 6

7. What did the bird do?

Write the answer and colour in

_____

_____

_____

COMPETITION TIME!

Watch the Juz 6 episode for the questions

Circle the correct answer

Each correct answer is worth 2 points, leaving you with a total score out of 6

Lets see if you can beat The Azharis!

Question	Answer (Circle the correct answer)		Score
1	Musa	Eesa	
2	Right	Left	
3	Hawaa	Hajr	
	Total Score		/6

JUZ 6

THE AZHARI PAD

Watch the Juz 6 episode for the questions

Draw: 1. An animal that is white and has horns. 2. Your favourite cake.

The Azharis | Juz by Juz Stories 29

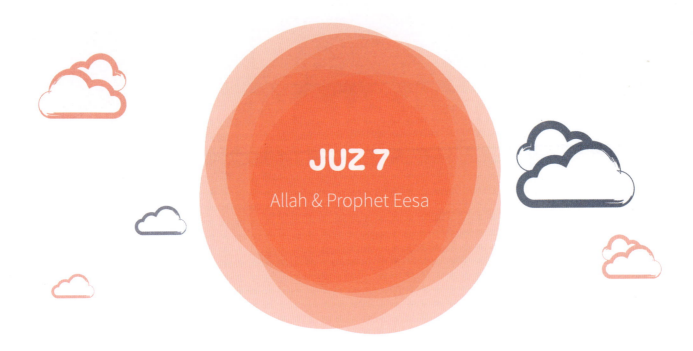

JUZ 7
Allah & Prophet Eesa

1. What is a ma'idah?

Break the code | Refer to the code breaker sheet at the end of the workbook

___ ___ ___ ___ ___ ___ ___ ___ ___

___ ___ ___ ___

2. What is a witness?

Write the answer and colour in

_____
_____
_____

3. How many angels write our deeds?

Circle the correct answer

1　　　2　　　3

Wordsearch

Tick off the words as you find them

○ ALLAH
○ EESA
○ IHSAN
○ FIRE

S	A	L	L	A	H
F	D	A	R	K	F
P	E	E	S	A	I
R	J	C	M	M	R
I	H	S	A	N	E
G	C	F	B	I	D

JUZ 7

4. What does Ar Raqeeb mean?

Write the answer

_____

_____

_____

_____

COMPETITION TIME!

Watch the Juz 7 episode for the questions

Circle the correct answer

Each correct answer is worth 2 points, leaving you with a total score out of 6

Lets see if you can beat The Azharis!

Question	Answer (Circle the correct answer)		Score
1	Musa	Eesa	
2	Nuh	Idris	
3	Bilal	Abu Bakr	
	Total Score		/6

JUZ 7

THE AZHARI PAD

Watch the Juz 7 episode for the questions

Draw: 1. In Mecca when we do tawaf what do we go around? **2.** Something you made dua for.

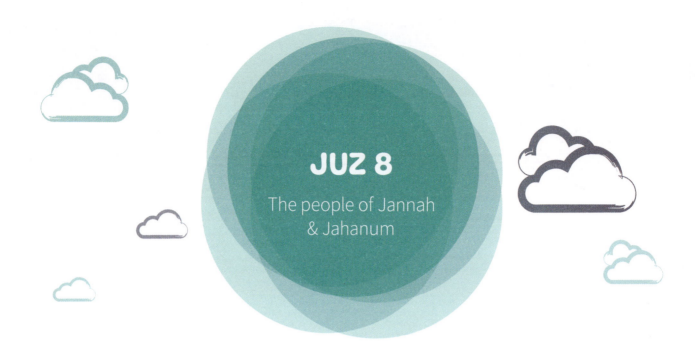

JUZ 8
The people of Jannah & Jahanum

1. Draw an example of a good deed.

Draw

2. The people of A'raaf are those whose _____ _____ equal their _____ _____ .

Fill in the gaps

3. Give an example of what we can do to get to Jannah.
Join the dots and colour in

4. Ramadan is the month of?
Find your way to the correct answer

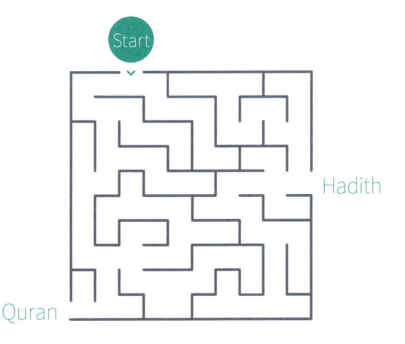

JUZ 8

5. What is the name of the extra prayer in Ramadan?

Break the code | Refer to the code breaker sheet at the end of the workbook

___ ___ ___ ___ ___ ___ ___

_____

COMPETITION TIME!

Watch the Juz 8 episode for the questions

Circle the correct answer

Each correct answer is worth 2 points, leaving you with a total score out of 6

Lets see if you can beat The Azharis!

Question	Answer (Circle the correct answer)		Score
1	Idris	Harun	
2	Ibrahim	Eesa	
3	Yusuf	Yaqub	
Total Score			/6

  JUZ 8

The Azharis | Juz by Juz Stories 36

THE AZHARI PAD

Watch the Juz 8 episode for the questions

1

2

Draw: 1. If there are 2 houses, draw what is between the houses. 2. What you would like to eat in Jannah?

JUZ 9
Prophet Musa & the magicians

1. What was the name of the bad person Prophet Musa was sent to?

Unscramble the letters below

WIRAFN

_____

2. How many magicians do you think were called?

Circle the correct answer

70,000   10,000   30,000

3. Who was with Musa?

Write the answer

_____

4. Who threw their stick first?

Colour in the correct answer

MAGICIANS

MUSA

5. What did the staff of Prophet Musa do?

Write the answer and colour in

_____

_____

_____

6. What did the magicians do when they were worried?

Complete the dot to dot and write the answer

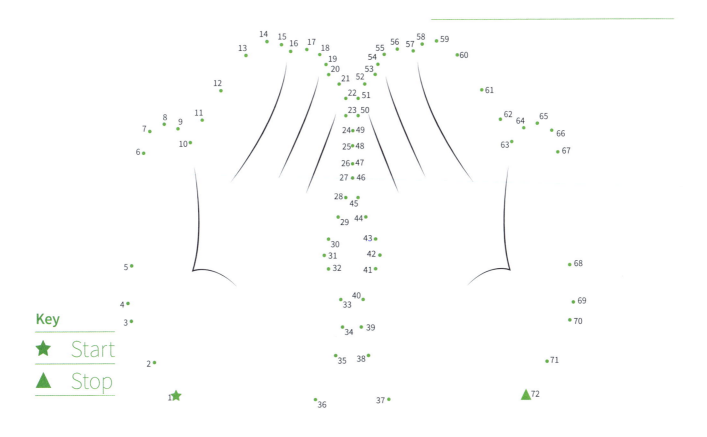

Key

★ Start

▲ Stop

JUZ 9

7. What is sajdah?

Write the answer and colour in

_____

_____

_____

COMPETITION TIME!

Watch the Juz 9 episode for the questions

Circle the correct answer

Each correct answer is worth 2 points, leaving you with a total score out of 6

Lets see if you can beat The Azharis!

Question	Answer (Circle the correct answer)		Score
1	Dates	Bread	
2	Surah Al Ikhlas	Surah An Nas	
3	Left	Right	
Total Score			/6

  JUZ 9

THE AZHARI PAD

Watch the Juz 9 episode for the questions

Draw: 1. Something you do on Eid day. 2. The animal that the sticks looked like they turned into.

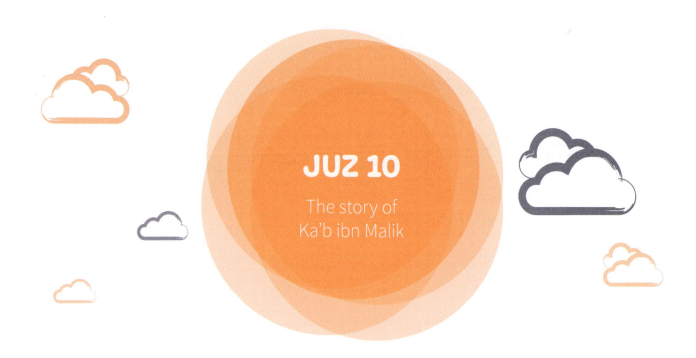

JUZ 10
The story of Ka'b ibn Malik

1. Who was whispering to Ka'b?

Write the answer

_____

2. Which surah does Allah say Shaytan whispers to us in?

Join the dots

SURAH
AN NAS

3. Is it good to lie?

Colour in the correct answer

YES | NO

4. When we make a mistake what should we do?

Write the answer

_____
_____
_____

5. How many nights was Ka'b alone for?

Circle the correct answer

30   50   70

6. Who ran between mounts Safa and Marwa?

Unscramble the letters below

JRAAH

_____

Wordsearch

Tick off the words as you find them

○ HAJAR
○ SAFA
○ MARWA
○ KAB

H	S	K	A	H	I
M	A	R	W	A	T
E	F	J	A	S	P
W	A	C	A	M	K
A	H	S	W	R	A
D	C	S	S	K	B

JUZ 10

7. When Ka'b was so happy, what did he do?

Write the answer and colour in

_____

_____

_____

COMPETITION TIME!

Watch the Juz 10 episode for the questions

Circle the correct answer

Each correct answer is worth 2 points, leaving you with a total score out of 6

Lets see if you can beat The Azharis!

Question	Answer (Circle the correct answer)		Score
1	Maghrib	Isha	
2	Before Fajr	Before Dhuhr	
3	Left	Right	
	Total Score		/6

JUZ 10

THE AZHARI PAD

Watch the Juz 10 episode for the question

1

Draw: 1. If you had to cross a desert, what would you pack in your bag?

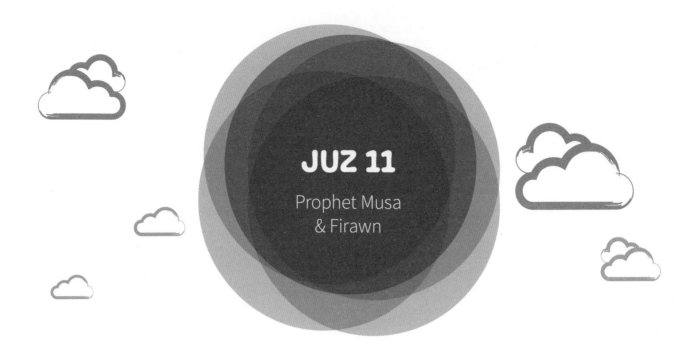

JUZ 11
Prophet Musa & Firawn

1. Which country was Prophet Musa in?

Write the answer and colour in

_____

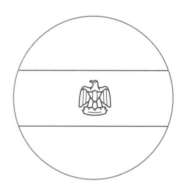

2. When did Prophet Musa leave with his people?

Circle the correct answer

Day   Night

3. What is the dua for leaving your house?

Colour in

Bismillah tawakaltu ala Allah wa la hawla wa la quwatta illa billah
(Tirmidhi)

4. How many horses did Firawn have?

Circle the correct answer and colour in

1,000

10,000

100,000

5. What does it mean to worship Allah?

Write the answer

_____

_____

_____

6. Did Firawn believe in Allah?

Find your way to the correct answer

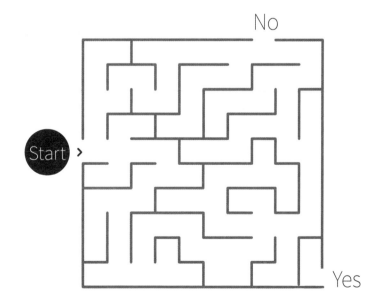

JUZ 11

7. Which month was the Quran revealed in?

Break the code | Refer to the code breaker sheet at the end of the workbook

__ __ __ __ __ __ __

_____

COMPETITION TIME!

Watch the Juz 11 episode for the questions

Circle the correct answer

Each correct answer is worth 2 points, leaving you with a total score out of 6

Lets see if you can beat The Azharis!

Question	Answer (Circle the correct answer)		Score
1	2	4	
2	Left	Right	
3	Right	Left	
Total Score			/6

JUZ 11

THE AZHARI PAD

Watch the Juz 11 episode for the questions

1

2

Draw: 1. The tallest thing you can think of. **2.** In Ramadan what can we do to worship Allah?

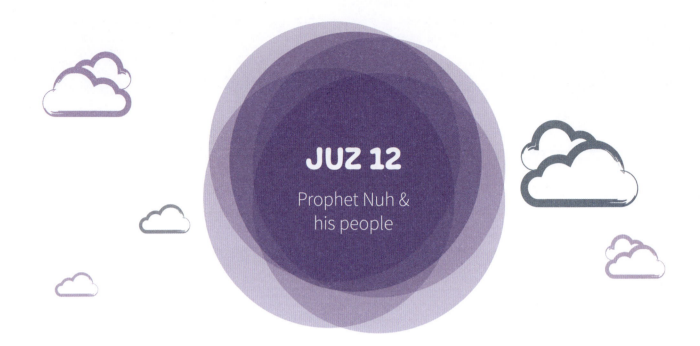

1. What is an ark?

Write the answer and colour in

_____

_____

_____

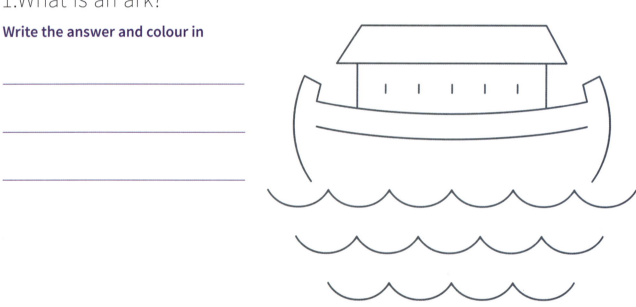

2. How many levels did the ark have?

Circle the correct answer

3   5   9   6   2

3. Did Prophet Nuh's people listen when he told them to ask for forgiveness?

Colour in the correct answer

YES | NO

4. Lots of _____ fell down from the _____ .

Fill in the gaps and colour in

5. Where did Prophet Nuh's people put their fingers in?

Complete the dot to dot and write the answer

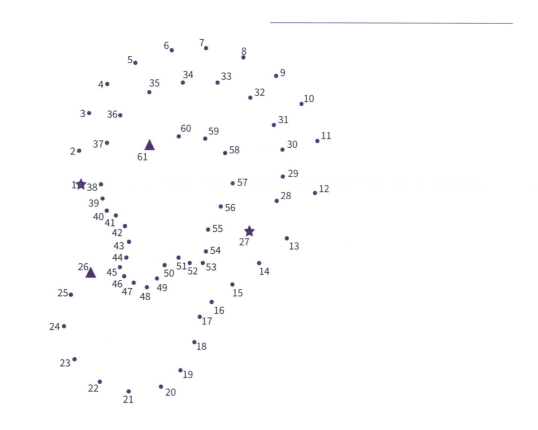

Key

★ Start
▲ Stop

6. Where did Prophet Nuh's son say he would go?

Unscramble the words below

A TONUMAIN

___ _____

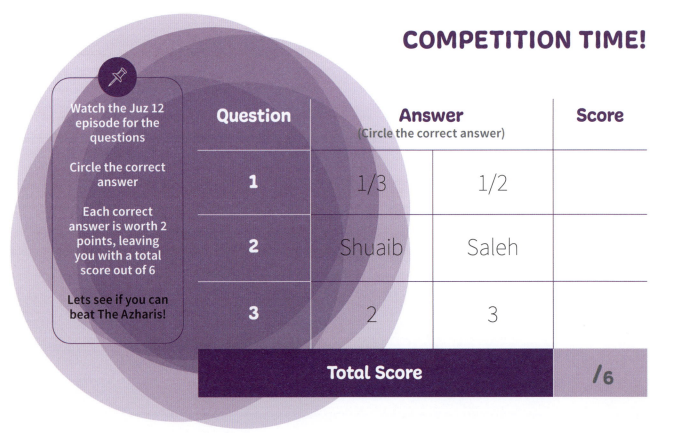

COMPETITION TIME!

Watch the Juz 12 episode for the questions

Circle the correct answer

Each correct answer is worth 2 points, leaving you with a total score out of 6

Lets see if you can beat The Azharis!

Question	Answer (Circle the correct answer)		Score
1	1/3	1/2	
2	Shuaib	Saleh	
3	2	3	
Total Score			/6

JUZ 12

THE AZHARI PAD

Watch the Juz 12 episode for the questions

1

2

Draw: 1. Your favourite animal. 2. Your favourite food.

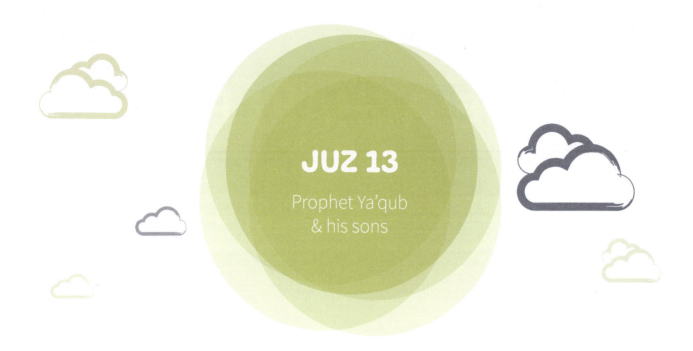

JUZ 13
Prophet Ya'qub & his sons

1. What was the name of the Prophet who was thrown into the well?

Circle the correct answer

Yunus   Yusuf   Yahya

2. Is it light or dark outside at the time for Isha?

Write the answer and colour in

_____

3. What animal did they say ate Yusuf?
Complete the dot to dot and write the answer

_____

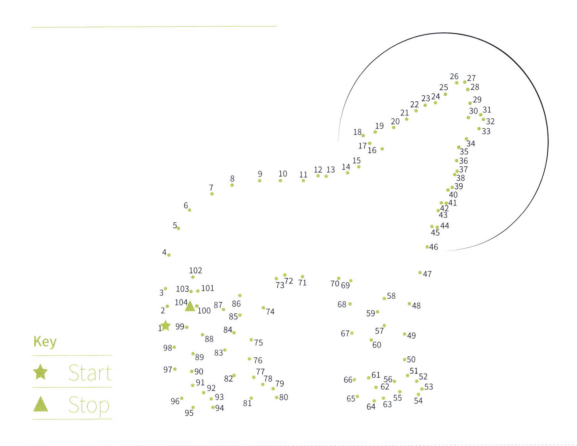

Key
★ Start
▲ Stop

4. What was the name of Prophet Yusuf's younger brother?
Colour in the correct answer

5. How do we make dua?
Write the answer

_____
_____
_____
_____

JUZ 13

6. Which hand do we eat with?
Write the answer and colour in

_____

7. What do we say before starting anything?
Trace the dots

BISMILLAH

COMPETITION TIME!

Watch the Juz 13 episode for the questions

Circle the correct answer

Each correct answer is worth 2 points, leaving you with a total score out of 6

Lets see if you can beat The Azharis!

Question	Answer		Score
	(Circle the correct answer)		
1	Mecca	Medinah	
2	Yes	No	
3	Mecca	Masjid Al Aqsa	
Total Score			/6

  JUZ 13

THE AZHARI PAD

Watch the Juz 13 episode for the question

Draw 1. What do you think Prophet Yusuf's shirt would look like?

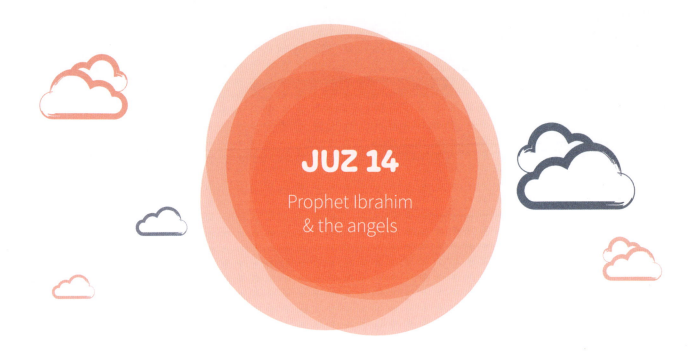

JUZ 14
Prophet Ibrahim & the angels

1. How many angels came to him?

Circle the correct answer

6   10   3

2. What did they say to greet him?

Break the code | Refer to the code breaker sheet at the end of the workbook

_ _ _ _ _ _ _ _ _ _ _ _ _ _ _

3. The angels did _____ eat the _____ .

Fill in the gaps and colour in

4. Write an example of being kind?

Write the answer

_____

_____

_____

Wordsearch

Tick off the words as you find them

○ ANGEL
○ FOOD
○ LAMB
○ KIND

F	M	L	A	D	S
T	A	R	O	L	K
L	I	O	R	E	I
A	F	N	A	G	N
M	F	S	G	N	D
B	F	A	L	A	C

JUZ 14

5. Why do we send salaam upon Prophet Ibrahim when we pray?
Write the answer

COMPETITION TIME!

Watch the Juz 14 episode for the questions

Circle the correct answer

Each correct answer is worth 2 points, leaving you with a total score out of 6

Lets see if you can beat The Azharis!

Question	Answer		Score
	(Circle the correct answer)		
1	Dhuhr	Asr	
2	63	83	
3	Yusuf	Musa	
Total Score			/6

JUZ 14

THE AZHARI PAD

Watch the Juz 14 episode for the questions

Draw: 1. The animal you think it was. 2. How old do you think Prophet Ibrahim was then?

JUZ 15
Prophet Musa & Khidr

1. What is a khutbah?

Write the answer

_____

_____

2. What was the name of the young boy?

Colour in

YUSHA

3. Which colour in Arabic is Khudra?

Trace the dots

GREEN

4. He was called Khidr because wherever he went the _____ turned _____ .

Fill in the gaps

5. What did Khidr make a hole in?

Complete the dot to dot and write the answer

Key
★ Start
▲ Stop

6. What was the condition for Prophet Musa to follow Khidr?

Write the answer

_____

_____

_____

JUZ 15

7. When you help others, what will Allah do?

Break the code | Refer to the code breaker sheet at the end of the workbook

_____ _____ _____ _____   _____ _____ _____

_____

COMPETITION TIME!

Watch the Juz 15 episode for the questions

Circle the correct answer

Each correct answer is worth 2 points, leaving you with a total score out of 6

Lets see if you can beat The Azharis!

Question	Answer		Score
	(Circle the correct answer)		
1	Aisha	Mariam	
2	Dhuhr	Fajr	
3	2	3	
Total Score			/6

   JUZ 15

THE AZHARI PAD

Watch the Juz 15 episode for the questions

Draw: 1. Something we normally eat with chips. 2. Something a pirate would bury.

The Azharis | Juz by Juz Stories 65

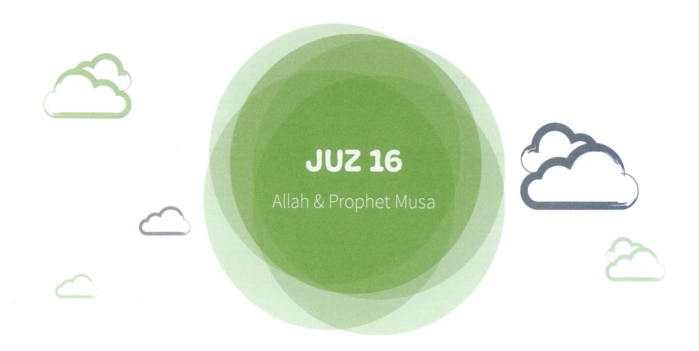

JUZ 16
Allah & Prophet Musa

1. What did they use to tell directions at the time of Prophet Musa?

Complete the dot to dot and write the answer

_____

Key

★ Start

▲ Stop

2. What was Prophet Musa told to take off?

Write the answer and colour in

_____

3. Is lying good or bad?

Colour in the correct answer

4. Firawn was in charge of which country?

Write the answer

_____

5. What happened to Prophet Musa's tongue when he was a baby?

Write the answer

_____

_____

JUZ 16

6. Who was Prophet Musa's brother?

Circle the correct answer

Harun   Dawud   Sulaiman

COMPETITION TIME!

Watch the Juz 16 episode for the questions

Circle the correct answer

Each correct answer is worth 2 points, leaving you with a total score out of 6

Lets see if you can beat The Azharis!

Question	Answer		Score
	(Circle the correct answer)		
1	2	4	
2	SubhanAllah	Alhamdulilah	
3	Arabic	English	
Total Score			/6

JUZ 16

THE AZHARI PAD

Watch the Juz 16 episode for the questions

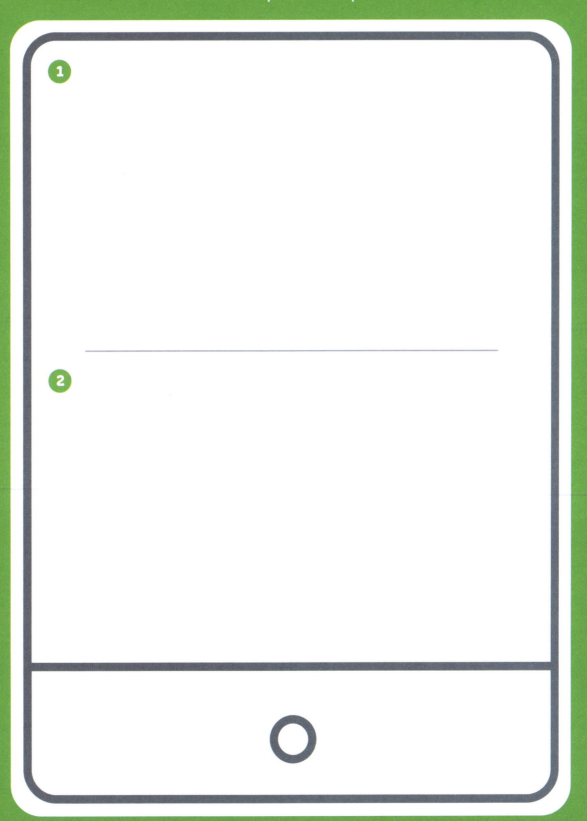

Draw: 1. What was in his hand? **2.** A picture of something we break our fast with in Ramadan.

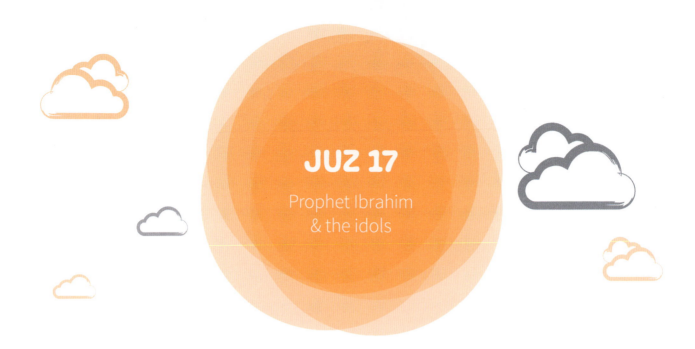

JUZ 17
Prophet Ibrahim & the idols

1. How old was Prophet Ibrahim when he played with the statues?

Write the answer

_____

2. His dad would say, the ears of the statue were _____ which meant they know _____ .

Fill in the gaps

3. What did Prophet Ibrahim use to break them?

Break the code | Refer to the code breaker sheet at the end of the workbook

___ ___ ___

4. Can statues speak?

Find your way to the correct answer

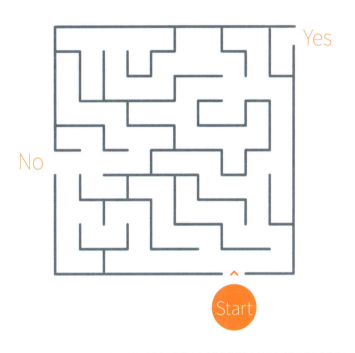

5. How did they put Prophet Ibrahim in the fire?

Trace the dots

They used a

CATAPULT

6. Which other Prophet used a catapult?

Unscramble the letters below

WUDAD

_____

7. Which angel came to Prophet Ibrahim?

Circle the correct answer

Jibril   Mikail   Israfil

COMPETITION TIME!

Watch the Juz 17 episode for the questions

Circle the correct answer

Each correct answer is worth 2 points, leaving you with a total score out of 6

Lets see if you can beat The Azharis!

Question	Answer (Circle the correct answer)		Score
1	Allah forgive me	Allah hears everything	
2	Muharram	Ramadan	
3	Zakah	Hajj	
	Total Score		/6

  JUZ 17

THE AZHARI PAD

Watch the Juz 17 episode for the questions

Draw: 1. When you think of Eid what comes to mind? **2.** What was Prophet Ibrahim thrown into?

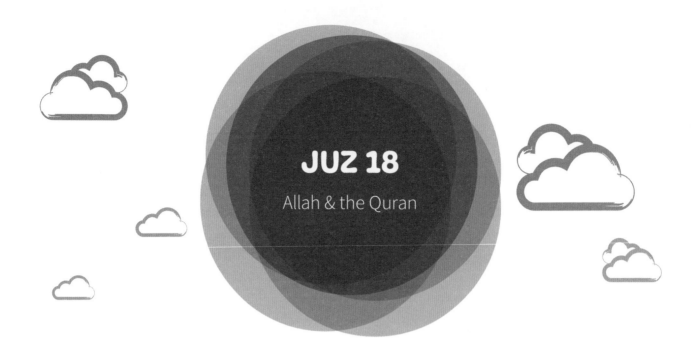

JUZ 18
Allah & the Quran

1. What part of your body is curved?

Write the answer

_____

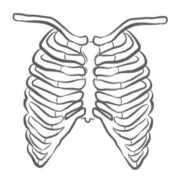

2. The Quran gives light to our heart?

Colour in the correct answer

TRUE

FALSE

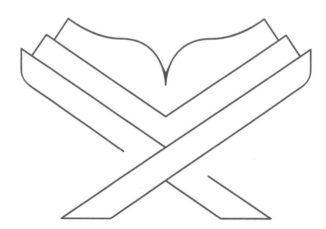

3. What did they use instead of light bulbs to see?

Complete the dot to dot and write the answer

_____

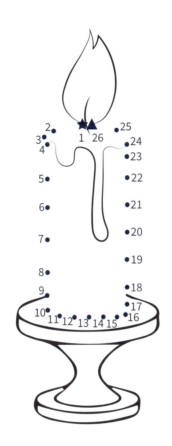

Key

★ Start

▲ Stop

4. How many times do we pray a day?

Circle the correct answer

3   5   1   7   9

5. What should we do if we find the Quran hard?

Unscramble the letters below

PTECRICA

_____

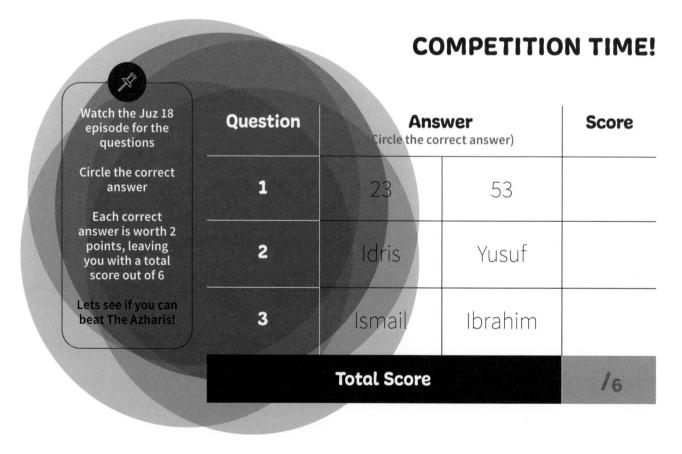

COMPETITION TIME!

Watch the Juz 18 episode for the questions

Circle the correct answer

Each correct answer is worth 2 points, leaving you with a total score out of 6

Lets see if you can beat The Azharis!

Question	Answer (Circle the correct answer)		Score
1	23	53	
2	Idris	Yusuf	
3	Ismail	Ibrahim	
Total Score			/6

JUZ 18

THE AZHARI PAD

Watch the Juz 18 episode for the questions

Draw: 1. A good deed you have done recently. 2. A picture of something you eat at breakfast.

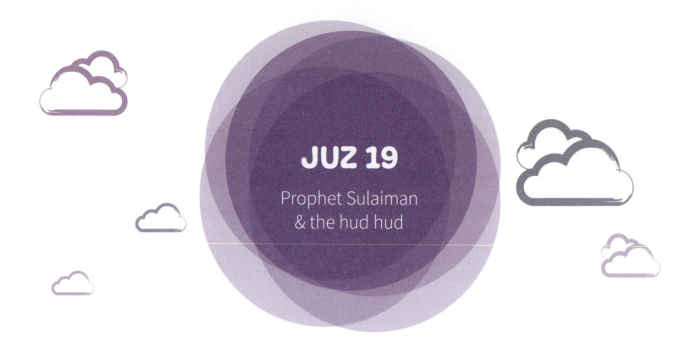

JUZ 19
Prophet Sulaiman & the hud hud

1. What could Prophet Sulaiman control?
Unscramble the letters below

SNIMALA

_____

2. What gives light from the sky?
Break the code | Refer to the code breaker sheet at the end of the workbook

___ ___ ___

3. Before we start anything, writing, _____ and drinking we should say _____.

Fill in the gaps

4. What is the dua after eating?
Colour in

الْحَمْدُ لِلَّهِ الَّذِي أَطْعَمَنِي هَذَا

وَرَزَقَنِيهِ مِنْ غَيْرِ حَوْلٍ مِنِّي وَلَا قُوَّةٍ

Alhumdu lillahi at amani hadha wa razaqanihi min ghayri hawlin minni wa la quwwatin
(Abu Dawud)

5. Is it sunnah to give gifts and presents?

Find your way to the correct answer

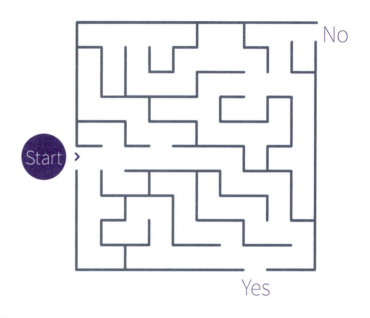

6. Draw an animal in the army of Prophet Sulaiman?

Draw

7. Before we go to sleep what should we recite?

Colour in

JUZ 19

8. What was the name of the Queen in the story?

Write the answer

_____

_____

COMPETITION TIME!

Watch the Juz 19 episode for the questions

Circle the correct answer

Each correct answer is worth 2 points, leaving you with a total score out of 6

Lets see if you can beat The Azharis!

Question	Answer (Circle the correct answer)		Score
1	Charity	Quran	
2	Mikail	Jibril	
3	Hajar	Houda	
	Total Score		/6

JUZ 19

THE AZHARI PAD

Watch the Juz 19 episode for the question

1

2

Draw: 1. Your favourite animal. **2.** What you think Kings and Queens sit on?

JUZ 20
Prophet Musa's Mother

1. Who had the dream of the fire?
Write the answer and colour in

_____

2. What was the name of the river Prophet Musa was put in?
Colour in

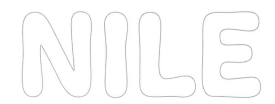

3. If you give in charity will Allah give you more back?
Circle the correct answer

YES   NO

4. When we speak to people how should we speak?
Break the code | Refer to the code breaker sheet at the end of the workbook

__ __ __ __ __ __

5. What happens when a parent makes dua for their child?
Write the answer

6. Who went to look for Prophet Musa after he was in the basket?
Write the answer and colour in

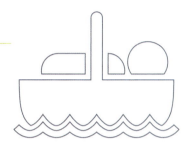

Wordsearch

Tick off the words as you find them

○ ALLAH
○ MUSA
○ NILE
○ CHILD

C	H	I	L	D	A
A	A	R	W	A	N
E	L	A	A	C	S
N	I	L	E	M	E
M	U	S	A	R	H
B	A	L	N	H	M

JUZ 20

7. What was the name of Firawn's wife?

Trace the dots

ASIYAH

COMPETITION TIME!

Watch the Juz 20 episode for the questions

Circle the correct answer

Each correct answer is worth 2 points, leaving you with a total score out of 6

Lets see if you can beat The Azharis!

Question	Answer		Score
	(Circle the correct answer)		
1	Hawaa	Hajar	
2	Zakariyah	Eesa	
3	Muhammad ﷺ	Eesa	
Total Score			/6

JUZ 20

THE AZHARI PAD

Watch the Juz 20 episode for the questions

Draw 1. What did Prophet Musa's Mother put him into?

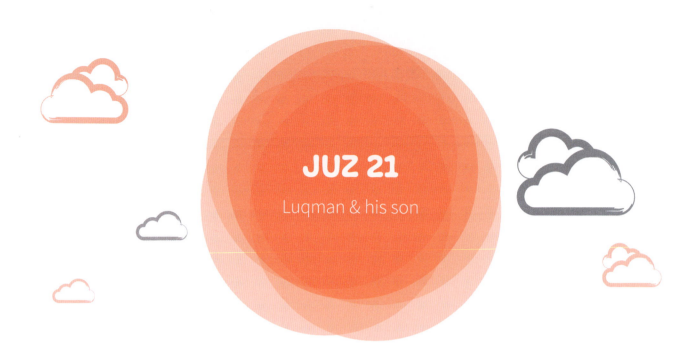

JUZ 21
Luqman & his son

1. The man who bought Luqman ordered him to slaughter a sheep and bring its worst part to him. Luqman brought the _____ and the _____ of the sheep to him.

Fill in the gaps and colour in

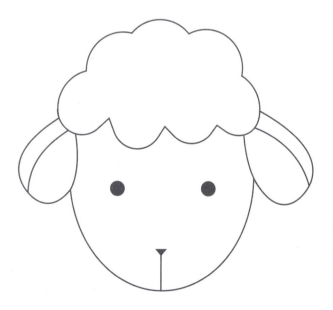

2. Should we make dua for our parents?

Colour in the correct answer

YES | NO

3. What does being arrogant mean?

Write the answer

_____
_____
_____
_____

4. Who thought they were better than Prophet Adam?

Trace the dots

SHAYTAN

Wordsearch

Tick off the words as you find them

- ◯ DUA
- ◯ ADAM
- ◯ HEART
- ◯ ISLAM

I	H	I	D	A	A
S	S	R	W	D	L
N	L	L	A	A	R
N	D	U	A	M	T
M	U	S	A	M	I
B	H	E	A	R	T

JUZ 21

5. What should we say when something good happens?

Unscramble the letters below

DHHAMAULILAL

_____

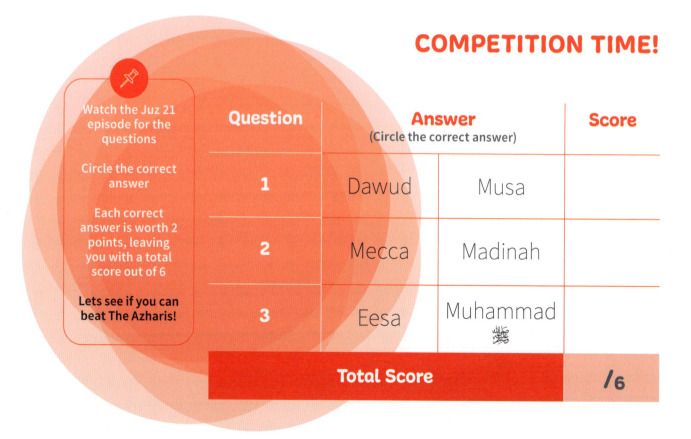

COMPETITION TIME!

Watch the Juz 21 episode for the questions

Circle the correct answer

Each correct answer is worth 2 points, leaving you with a total score out of 6

Lets see if you can beat The Azharis!

Question	Answer (Circle the correct answer)		Score
1	Dawud	Musa	
2	Mecca	Madinah	
3	Eesa	Muhammad ﷺ	
Total Score			/6

JUZ 21

THE AZHARI PAD

Watch the Juz 21 episode for the questions

Draw: 1. Your favourite toy. **2.** What was Shaytan made from?

The Azharis | Juz by Juz Stories 89

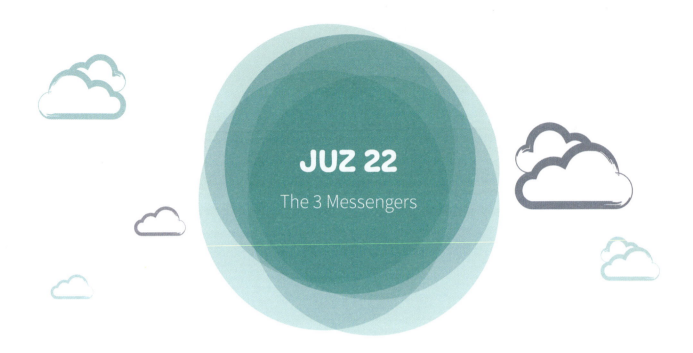

JUZ 22
The 3 Messengers

1. Give an example of when Allah sent two Prophets at the same time?
Write the answer

2. The most hated thing to the Prophet Muhammad ﷺ is lying?
Find your way to the correct answer

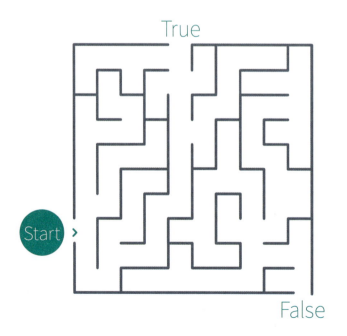

3. What is a drought?

Unscramble the words below and colour in

ON TAWRE

____ _____

4. Why do you think the man came running in the story?

Write the answer

_____

_____

_____

_____

_____

5. Where did the man go?

Colour in the correct answer

JANNAH

JAHANUM

6. What was the easy deed mentioned about Ramadan?

Break the code | Refer to the code breaker sheet at the end of the workbook

_ _ _ _ _ _ _   _ _ _ _

_____

COMPETITION TIME!

Watch the Juz 22 episode for the questions

Circle the correct answer

Each correct answer is worth 2 points, leaving you with a total score out of 6

Lets see if you can beat The Azharis!

Question	Answer (Circle the correct answer)		Score
1	Eesa	Yahya	
2	Left	Right	
3	Bilal	Umar	
	Total Score		/6

JUZ 22

THE AZHARI PAD

Watch the Juz 22 episode for the questions

Draw: 1. Something that flies in the sky. **2.** Something you would like to eat in Jannah.

JUZ 23
Prophets Ibrahim & Ismail

1. What was Prophet Ibrahim making dua for at the beginning?

Write the answer and colour in

_____

2. How old was Prophet Ibrahim when Allah answered his dua?

Circle the correct answer

86

42

100

3. Which other Prophet saw a dream of sun, moon and stars?

Unscramble the letters below

FUYSU

_____

4. Where did Ismail learn about Allah?

Complete the dot to dot and write the answer

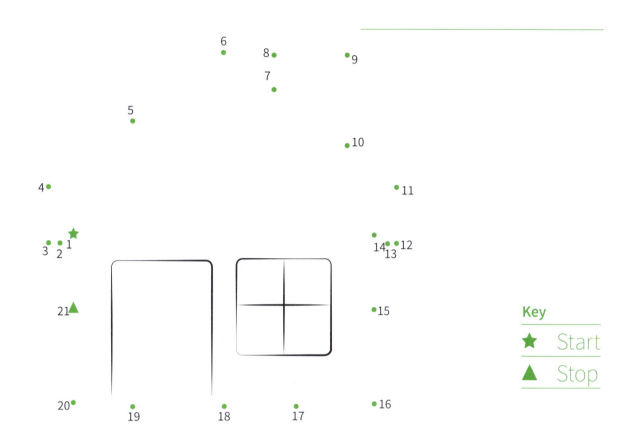

Key
★ Start
▲ Stop

5. When Shaytan came to Prophet _____ he threw 7 _____ at him.

Fill in the gaps and colour in

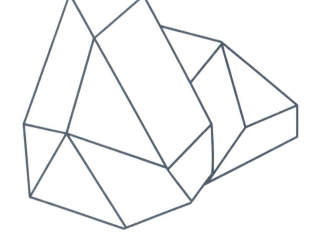

6. Is making dua a good deed?

Colour in the correct answer

YES | NO

COMPETITION TIME!

Watch the Juz 23 episode for the questions

Circle the correct answer

Each correct answer is worth 2 points, leaving you with a total score out of 6

Lets see if you can beat The Azharis!

Question	Answer		Score
	(Circle the correct answer)		
1	Monday	Friday	
2	Abu Bakr	Musa	
3	Yaqub	Yusha	
Total Score			/6

JUZ 23

THE AZHARI PAD

Watch the Juz 23 episode for the questions

Draw: 1. Something you would really like to ask Allah. 2. That animal.

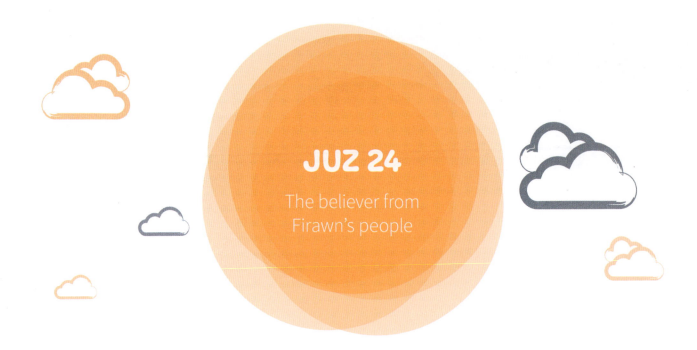

JUZ 24
The believer from Firawn's people

1. How was the man related to Firawn?

Circle the correct answer

His Cousin

His Brother

His Father

2. What are some of the things we should thank Allah for?

Write the answer

_____

_____

_____

_____

3. What can we say to thank Allah?

Break the code | Refer to the code breaker sheet at the end of the workbook

__ __ __ __ __ __ __ __ __ __ __ __

4. What happens when we thank Allah for something?

Write the answer and colour in

_____

_____

_____

Wordsearch

Tick off the words as you find them

○ SEA
○ MAN
○ QURAN
○ ISLAM

I	H	A	I	S	A
S	E	R	S	A	S
S	E	L	L	A	E
Q	U	R	A	N	A
M	U	S	M	M	I
Q	E	M	A	N	T

— JUZ 24 —

5. What happened to Firawn when he went into the sea?

Write the answer

_____

_____

_____

6. Was the cousin of Firawn saved?

Colour in the correct answer

YES | NO

COMPETITION TIME!

Watch the Juz 24 episode for the questions

Circle the correct answer

Each correct answer is worth 2 points, leaving you with a total score out of 6

Lets see if you can beat The Azharis!

Question	Answer		Score
	(Circle the correct answer)		
1	Monday	Friday	
2	3	4	
3	Cats	Sheep	
Total Score			/6

JUZ 24

THE AZHARI PAD

Watch the Juz 24 episode for the questions

1

2

Draw: 1. The animal. 2. A tower going into the sky.

The Azharis | Juz by Juz Stories 101

1. What did Prophet Ibrahim's people worship?

Find your way to the correct answer

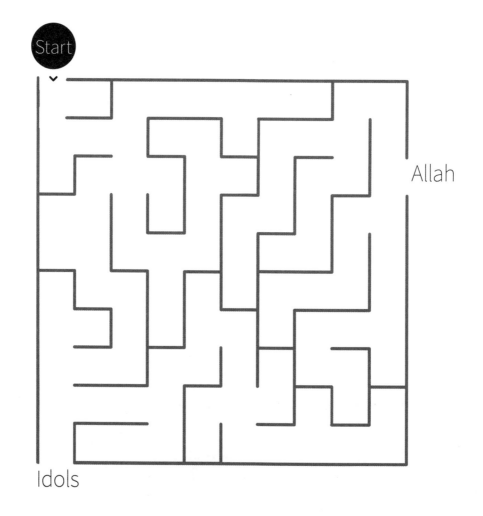

2. Was Prophet Muhammad ﷺ rich?

Write the answer and colour in

_____

3. Which angel came to Prophet Muhammad ﷺ in the story?

Unscramble the letters below

IJLRIB

_____

4. Before we go to bed what should we say?

Colour in

SUBHANALLAH

ALHAMDULILAH

ALLAHUAKBAR

JUZ 25

5. Who whispers to us and doesn't want us to concentrate in prayer?

Trace the dots

SHAYTAN

COMPETITION TIME!

Watch the Juz 25 episode for the questions

Circle the correct answer

Each correct answer is worth 2 points, leaving you with a total score out of 6

Lets see if you can beat The Azharis!

Question	Answer		Score
	(Circle the correct answer)		
1	Aisha	Khadijah	
2	Alhamdulilah	Bismillah	
3	33	100	
Total Score			/6

THE AZHARI PAD

Watch the Juz 25 episode for the questions

1

2

Draw: 1. What the Prophet Muhammad ﷺ slept on. 2. Somewhere you can go to do a good deed.

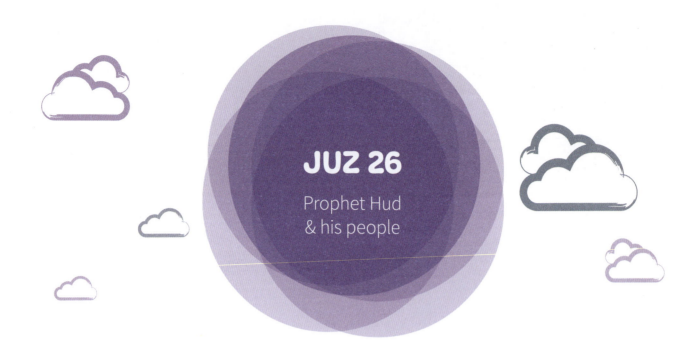

JUZ 26
Prophet Hud & his people

1. How do we ask Allah for forgiveness?

Write the answer

_____

_____

2. Were the people happy when they first saw the rain?

Colour in the correct answer

YES | NO

3. What is the dua before we enter the bathroom?

Colour in

Allaahumma innee a'oodhu bika minal-khubuthi wal-khabaa'ith
(Muslim)

4. The name of the last prayer at night is _____ and for it we read 4 rakah.

Fill in the gap and colour in

Wordsearch

Tick off the words as you find them

○ DUA
○ RAIN
○ ALLAH
○ ISHA

I	H	A	I	S	P
I	S	H	A	T	A
S	E	L	L	N	L
D	L	R	I	D	L
A	P	A	M	U	A
R	R	M	A	A	H

JUZ 26

5. What happened when the Jinns heard the Quran?

Write the answer

_____

_____

_____

COMPETITION TIME!

Watch the Juz 26 episode for the questions

Circle the correct answer

Each correct answer is worth 2 points, leaving you with a total score out of 6

Lets see if you can beat The Azharis!

Question	Answer (Circle the correct answer)		Score
1	Israfil	Mikail	
2	Ramadan	Muharram	
3	Abu Talib	Abdullah	
	Total Score		/6

JUZ 26

THE AZHARI PAD

Watch the Juz 26 episode for the questions

Draw: 1. If you lived in a desert, what would you need to live? 2. Something shiny in the sky.

JUZ 27
The hypocrites

1. What is the sirat?

Write the answer and colour in

_____

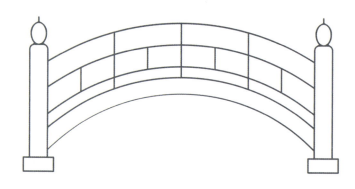

2. Who will tell the hypocrites to go back?

Unscramble the words below

NA GNAEL

___ _____

3. What gives life to our hearts?

Break the code | Refer to the code breaker sheet at the end of the workbook

___ ___ ___ ___ ___

4. What should we recite after every prayer?

Colour in

AYATUL KURSI

Wordsearch

Tick off the words as you find them

- ⭕ HAND
- ⭕ READ
- ⭕ ALLAH
- ⭕ HEART

A	L	L	A	H	R
H	E	A	R	T	L
R	E	L	D	H	S
A	L	A	I	A	L
H	E	A	M	N	T
R	A	N	A	D	P

  JUZ 27

5. What would the Prophet ﷺ do before bed?
Write the answer

_____

_____

_____

_____

———————————————

COMPETITION TIME!

Watch the Juz 27 episode for the questions

Circle the correct answer

Each correct answer is worth 2 points, leaving you with a total score out of 6

Lets see if you can beat The Azharis!

Question	Answer (Circle the correct answer)		Score
1	Amina	Khadijah	
2	Jummah	Dhuhr	
3	Left foot	Right foot	
	Total Score		/6

JUZ 27

The Azharis | Juz by Juz Stories 112

THE AZHARI PAD

Watch the Juz 27 episode for the questions

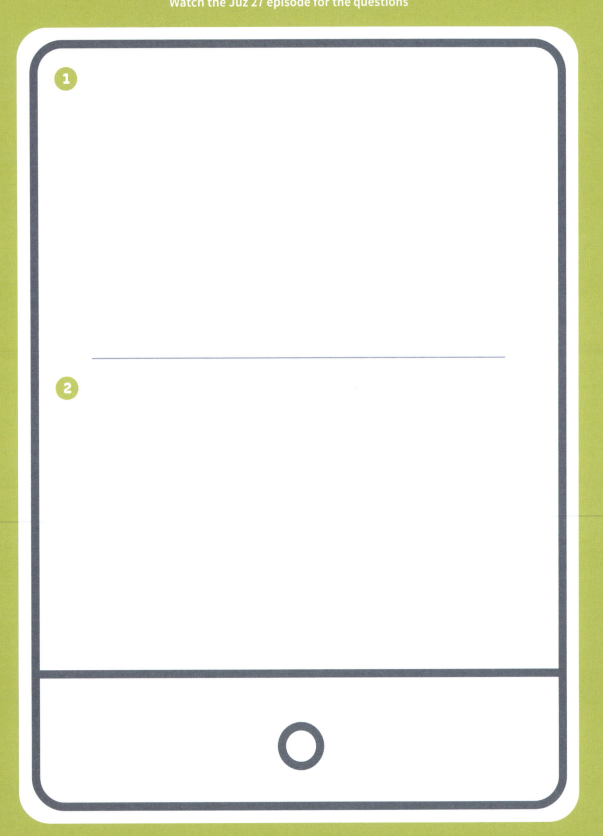

Draw: 1. What do you think your house will look like in Jannah? **2.** Something that grows up from soil.

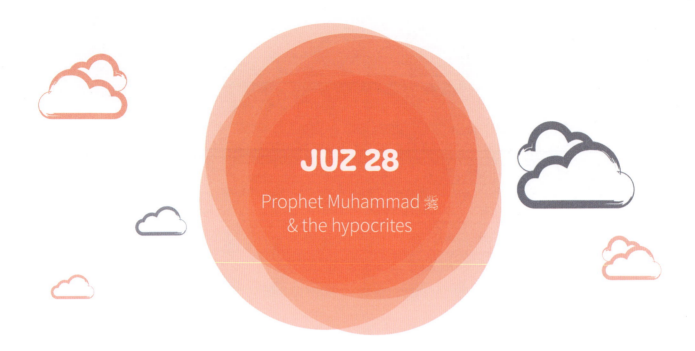

JUZ 28
Prophet Muhammad ﷺ & the hypocrites

1. What happened to the group of Muslims the Prophet Muhammad ﷺ sent?

Write the answer

_____

_____

2. What did they want to throw on the Prophet Muhammad ﷺ?

Complete the dot to dot and write the answer

_____

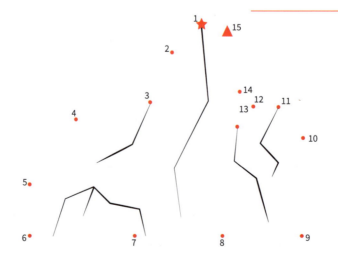

3. Who was the Prophet Muhammad ﷺ sitting with?

Circle the two correct answers

Abu Bakr

Bilal

Umar

Ali

4. Was the Prophet Muhammad ﷺ kind to them even after the Muslims won?

Colour in the correct answer

YES | NO

5. What did they use to travel?

Unscramble the letters below and colour in

CLEMA

_____

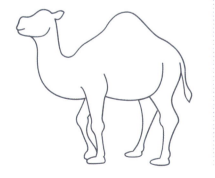

6. Did the hypocrites help when they said they would?

Trace the dots

JUZ 28

7. If you do something good and others follow, you get their good deeds as well.

True or False? Write the answer and colour in

_____

COMPETITION TIME!

Watch the Juz 28 episode for the questions

Circle the correct answer

Each correct answer is worth 2 points, leaving you with a total score out of 6

Lets see if you can beat The Azharis!

Question	Answer		Score
	(Circle the correct answer)		
1	Eesa	Muhammad ﷺ	
2	2	4	
3	Elephant	Rhino	
Total Score			/6

JUZ 28

THE AZHARI PAD

Watch the Juz 28 episode for the questions

1.

2.

Draw: 1. A house. 2. A picture to show what sadaqah is.

JUZ 29
Prophet Nuh & his people

1. What is the name of Prophet Adam's wife?
Join the dots

HAWAA

2. Who was the Prophet sent after him?
Find your way to the correct answer

Start

Musa

Nuh

3. What did the people of Prophet Nuh do with their clothes?

Write the answer

_____

_____

_____

_____

4. Istighfar means asking Allah for _____.

Fill in the gap and colour in

5. How many times would the Prophet Muhammad ﷺ ask Allah for forgiveness in a day?

Circle the correct answer

33   60   100   70   40   1000

JUZ 29

6. What did Prophet Nuh tell his sons to say?

Colour in

SUBHANALLAHI WA BIHAMDIHI

COMPETITION TIME!

Watch the Juz 29 episode for the questions

Circle the correct answer

Each correct answer is worth 2 points, leaving you with a total score out of 6

Lets see if you can beat The Azharis!

Question	Answer (Circle the correct answer)		Score
1	Mecca	Medina	
2	Yusuf	Eesa	
3	Cave Hira	Cave Thawr	
Total Score			/6

JUZ 29

THE AZHARI PAD

Watch the Juz 29 episode for the questions

1

2

Draw: 1. A hat. 2. If you say Subhanallahi wa bihamdihi, what do you think you do get in Jannah?

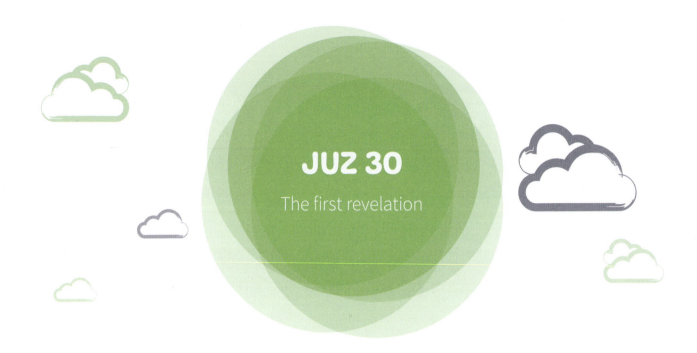

JUZ 30
The first revelation

1. What was the name of the cave?

Unscramble the words below

VACE   AIRH

____   ____

2. Which month did this happen in?

Colour in

3. What was the name of the angel?

Break the code | Refer to the code breaker sheet at the end of the workbook

____ ____ ____ ____ ____ ____

4. What do you get if you were about to tell a lie when joking but you don't tell it?

Write the answer and colour in

_____

Wordsearch

Tick off the words as you find them

- ⭕ RUB
- ⭕ CAVE
- ⭕ ALLAH
- ⭕ HEART

A	L	L	A	H	R
R	A	N	R	D	L
R	E	L	U	H	C
A	L	A	B	A	A
H	E	A	M	N	V
H	E	A	R	T	E

JUZ 30

5. The name Ar Rub means?

Circle the correct answer

The One who forgives | The One who sees everything | The One that looks after us

COMPETITION TIME!

Watch the Juz 30 episode for the questions

Circle the correct answer

Each correct answer is worth 2 points, leaving you with a total score out of 6

Lets see if you can beat The Azharis!

Question	Answer (Circle the correct answer)		Score
1	Alhamdulilah	Bismillah	
2	Salih	Eesa	
3	Sulaiman	Dawud	
	Total Score		/6

JUZ 30

THE AZHARI PAD

Watch the Juz 30 episode for the question

Draw: 1. Something that you keep in a jar.

ANSWERS

Episode 1 | Juz 1

1. Earth
2. Sneezed
3. Alhumdulilah
4. Sins fall off like leaves off a tree
5. Prophet Dawud
6. 100 Years
7. Prophet Adam had forgotten that he had given 60 years of his life to Prophet Dawud

Episode 2 | Juz 2

1. Make dua
2. Poor
3. No
4. It moved to be on top of the statues
5. 310 people
6. Prophet Dawud

Episode 3 | Juz 3

1. Bring the dead back to life
2. Sun
3. No
4. Donkey
5. 100 Years

Episode 4 | Juz 4

1. 8
2. Abu Bakr
3. Umar
4. The Prophet ﷺ fell asleep and an insect bit Abu Bakr
5. Monday

Episode 5 | Juz 5

1. Not to fish on Saturday
2. Allah
3. Friday
4. The tree cried
5. Yes
6. -
7. No

Episode 6 | Juz 6

1. Sabil
2. The fire did not touch the sacrifice
3. -
4. Doing things to the best of your ability
5. Not wanting someone to have something
6. Crow
7. Dug a hole and threw sand over the dead one

Episode 7 | Juz 7

1. Table with food
2. Someone that saw something
3. 2
4. The One that looks over us

Episode 8 | Juz 8

1. -
2. Good deeds equal their bad deeds
3. Pray
4. Quran
5. Taraweh

Episode 9 | Juz 9

1. Firawn
2. 70,000
3. Harun
4. Magicians
5. The staff turned into a snake
6. Make dua
7. Putting your head on the floor

Episode 10 | Juz 10

1. Shaytan
2. Surah An Nas
3. No
4. Ask Allah for forgivness
5. 50
6. Hajar
7. He gave the man his outer clothing

Episode 11 | Juz 11

1. Egypt
2. Night
3. -
4. 100,000
5. Pray to him
6. No
7. Ramadan

Episode 12 | Juz 12

1. A big ship with a cover on top
2. 3
3. No
4. Rain, sky
5. Ears
6. A mountain

Episode 13 | Juz 13

1. Yusuf
2. Dark
3. Wolf
4. Binyamin
5. Raise our hands
6. Right
7. Bismillah

Episode 14 | Juz 14

1. 3
2. Assalamualaykum
3. Not, food
4. -
5. He sent salaam to us when he met Prophet Muhammad ﷺ

Episode 15 | Juz 15

1. The talk the imam gives at the Jummah prayer
2. Yusha
3. Green
4. Ground, green
5. Ship
6. Not to ask questions
7. Help you